All About
DRAWING

Horses & Pets

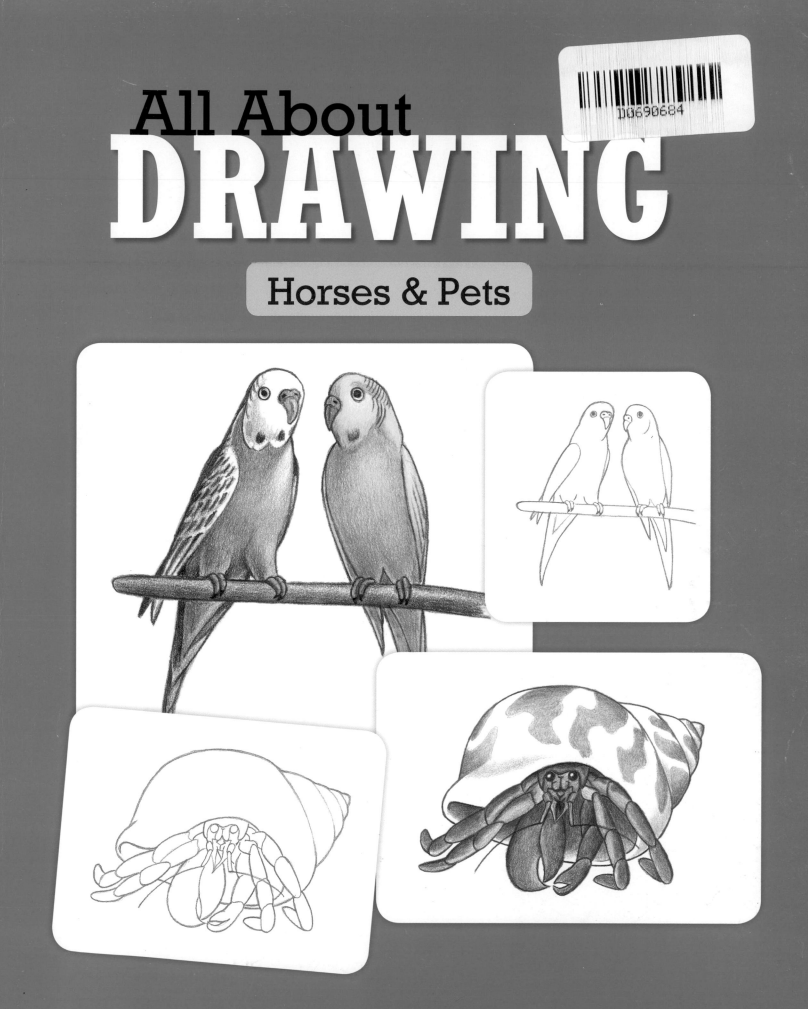

Illustrated by Russell Farrell and Peter Mueller

Getting Started

When you **look** closely at the **drawings** in this book, you'll notice that they're made up of basic shapes, such as circles, triangles, and rectangles. To draw all your favorite animal friends, just start with simple shapes as you see here. It's easy and fun!

Circles are used to draw heads, chests, and hips.

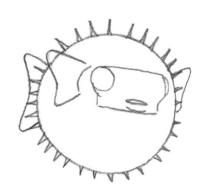

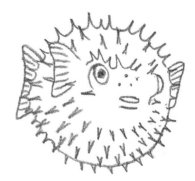

Ovals

make good profile heads and muzzles.

Triangles

are best for angled parts, like a snake's head.

FIND THE SHAPE!

Can you find circles, ovals, and triangles on these animals? Look closely at the dog's head and chest, and then check out the frog's body and angular legs. It's easy to see the basic shapes in any animal once you know what to look for!

Coloring Tips

There's more than one way to bring your **horse** and **pet** pals to life on paper—you can use colored pencils, crayons, markers, or watercolor. Just be sure you have plenty of natural colors—black, brown and gray, plus yellow, orange, and red.

Colored
pencil

Crayon

Pencil

Marker

Watercolor

With an assortment of horse breeds and pets to portray, the color possibilities are endless! Before you pick a coloring tool for your drawing, think about the animal's different textures. Is its skin furry, feathered, scaled, or smooth? Colored pencils have a sharp tip that is great for tiny details like small hairs and feathers. Crayons can be used to cover large areas quickly and markers make your colors appear more solid. Or try watercolor for a soft touch.

Puppy

This **lovable** Lab is a cute pup with a **chubby** body. Begin with an oval for the tummy and a circle for the head.

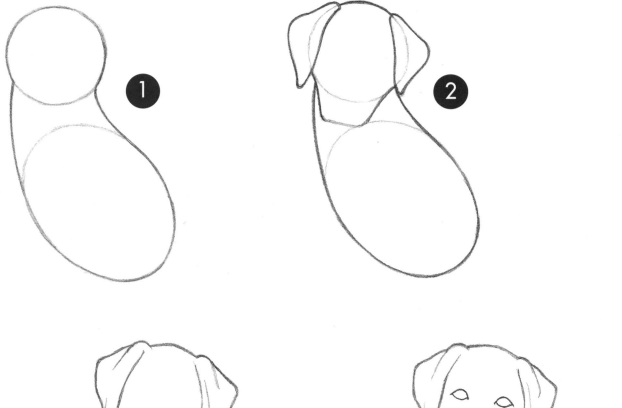

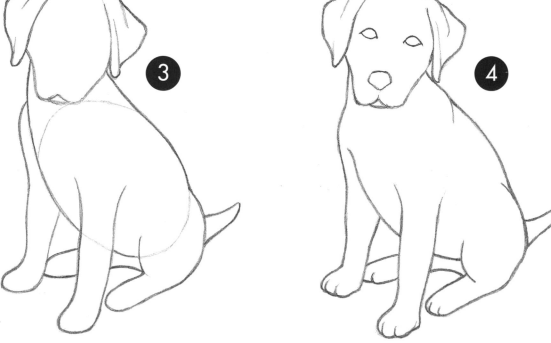

5

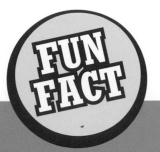

6

Kitten

This tiny **tabby** has a **fluffy** body and short, thick legs. Its round eyes and triangular ears look huge on its little furry frame!

5

6

Cats have excellent hearing and very flexible ears! They have 30 outer-ear muscles, which can rotate each ear a full 180 degrees. So felines can hear in all directions without moving their heads, which helps them pinpoint where sounds are coming from.

Hanoverian Foal

Start this **long-legged** baby with two circles for the body. Then finish with a short, brushlike tail and a stiff, upright mane.

Macaw

Use an oval to draw this **colorful, exotic** parrot's body. The bird's long feathers come to a point—so does its sharp, curved beak!

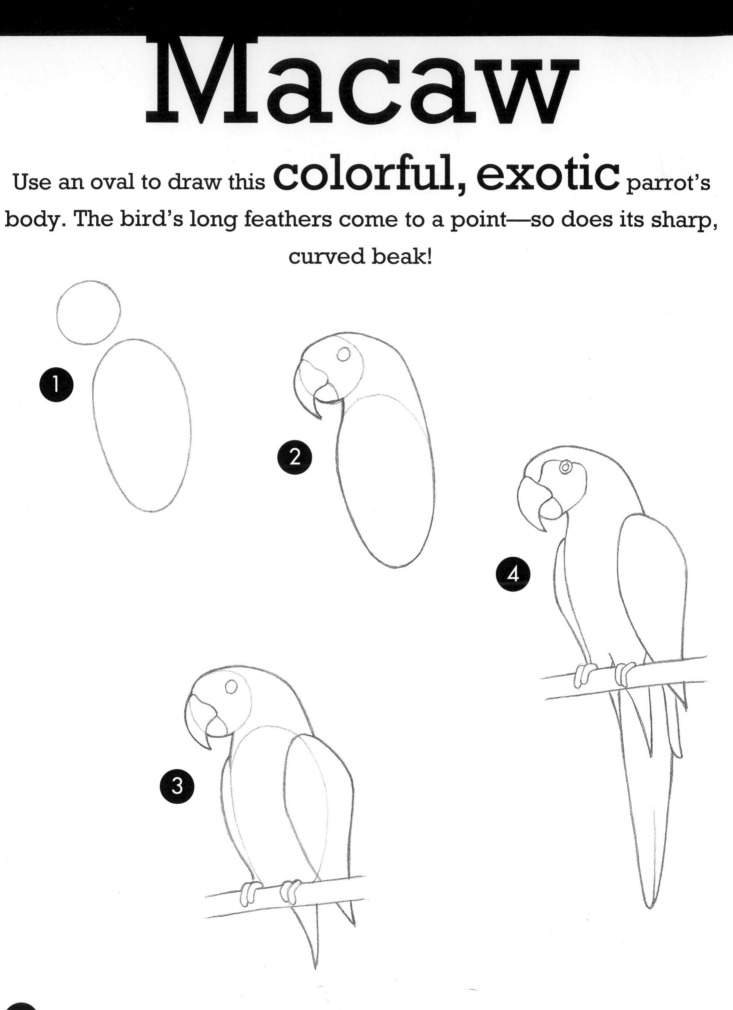

5

6

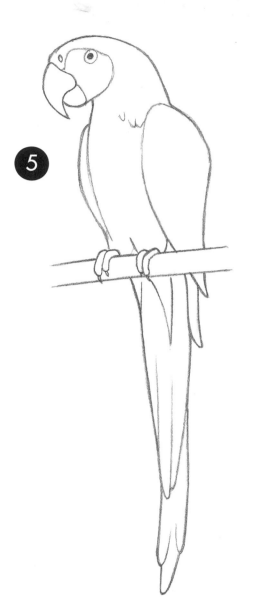

FUN FACT

A macaw's beak is so powerful it can easily crush a Brazil nut! And its dry, scaly tongue serves as a tool to break open and eat food.

Australian Pony

This **sweet** little pony from "down under" has a **fine,** delicate face and large, dark eyes. Say, "G'day, mate!"

Hackney Horse

This handsome **show horse** is strutting its stuff—
stretch out those legs and arch that tail high!

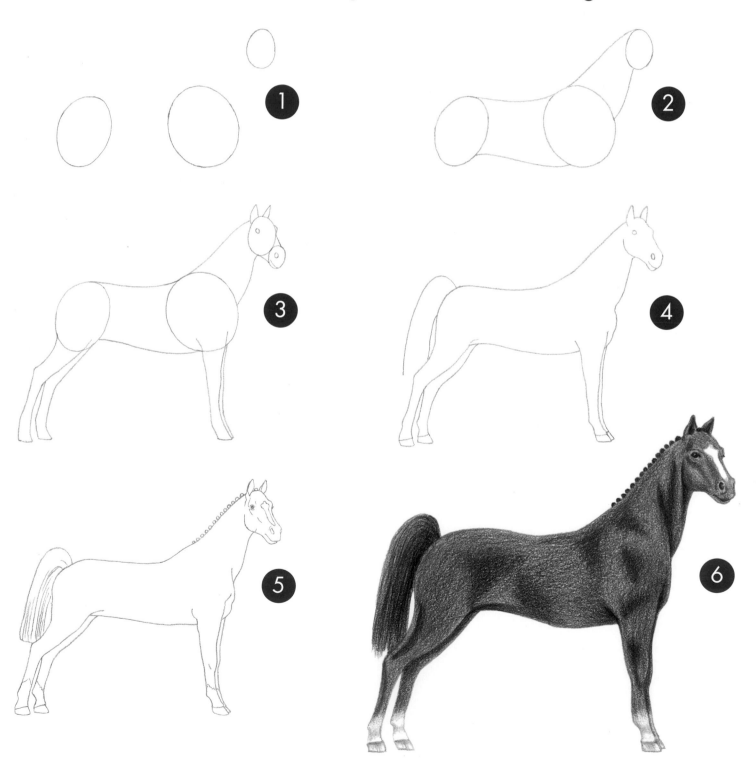

Bunny

This **Lop-eared** rabbit's body is **round,** but it isn't a perfect circle. Its long ears droop down, but its short tail swoops up!

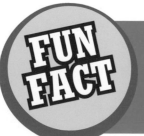

It's not unusual for caretakers to discover their pet bunnies fast asleep. After all, rabbits are *nocturnal,* which means they're active at night, so they sleep during the day. And, on average, rabbits take 16 naps per day to get in a full 8 hours of sleep!

Frog

It isn't easy being **green!** This **amphibian** has a few unusual features, like legs that fold and eyes that sit on top of its head!

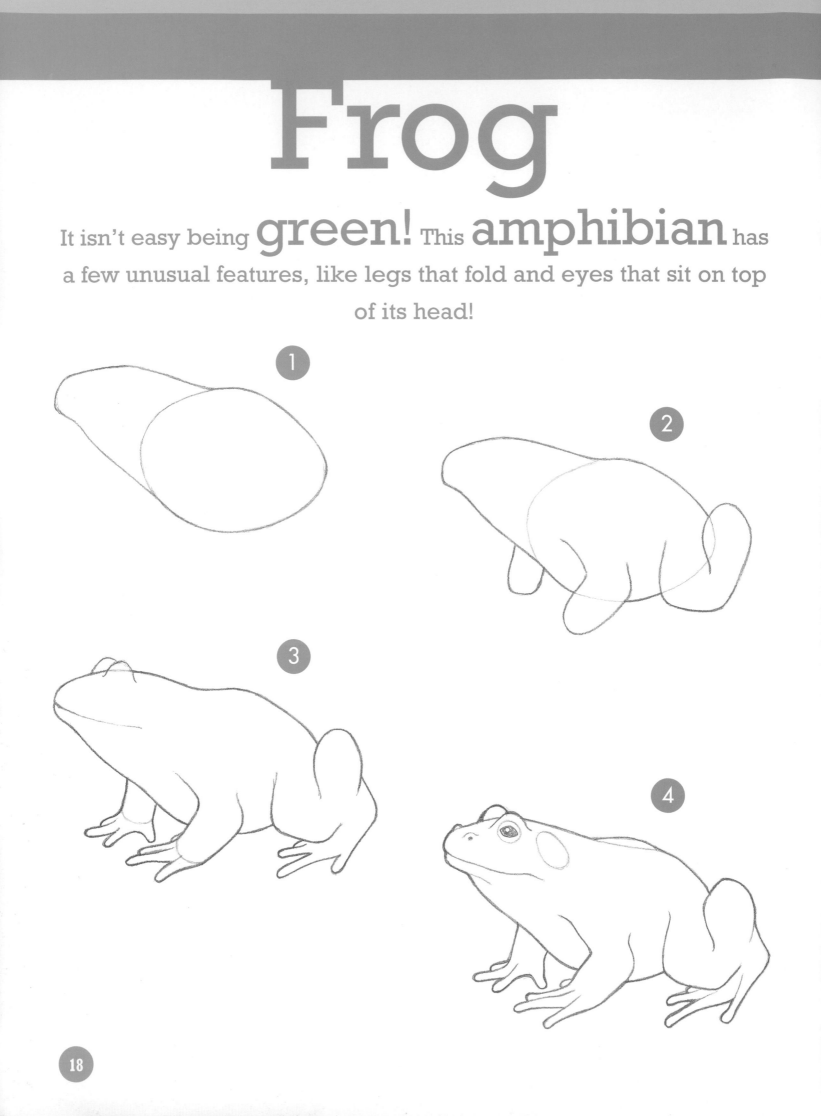

5

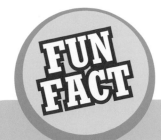

FUN FACT

There are a few species of frogs that can thaw out and return to life after being frozen. But don't try this at home! Since these frogs account for only a few of the 2,600 known frog species, you don't want to experiment on your hip-hopper!

FROGGY FACT

The tree frog usually keeps a low profile, blending in with the green leaves it lives on. But when threatened, it reveals its bold, red eyes and multicolored body to startle predators, before making a speedy escape.

Pinto

This **color** breed has a **cool** patterned coat that sets it apart! A Quarter Horse or Thoroughbred Pinto can also be called a "Paint."

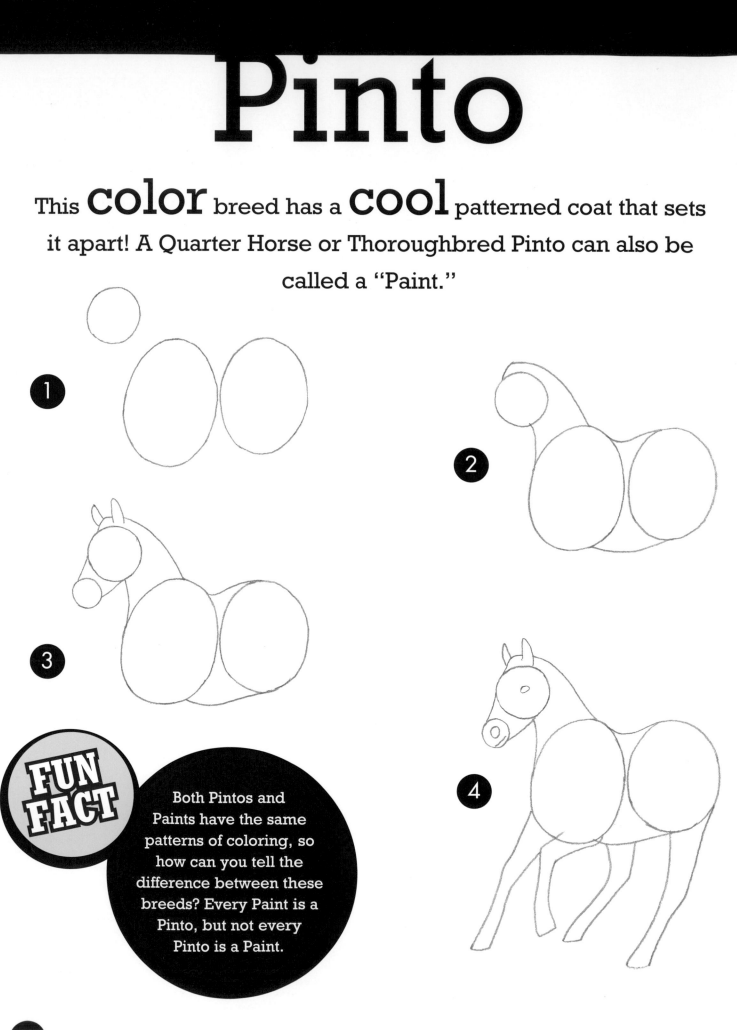

FUN FACT

Both Pintos and Paints have the same patterns of coloring, so how can you tell the difference between these breeds? Every Paint is a Pinto, but not every Pinto is a Paint.

Mouse

This **little** mammal has tiny **rodent** features: small, round eyes; a tiny pink nose; a long, thin tail; and itty, bitty toenails!

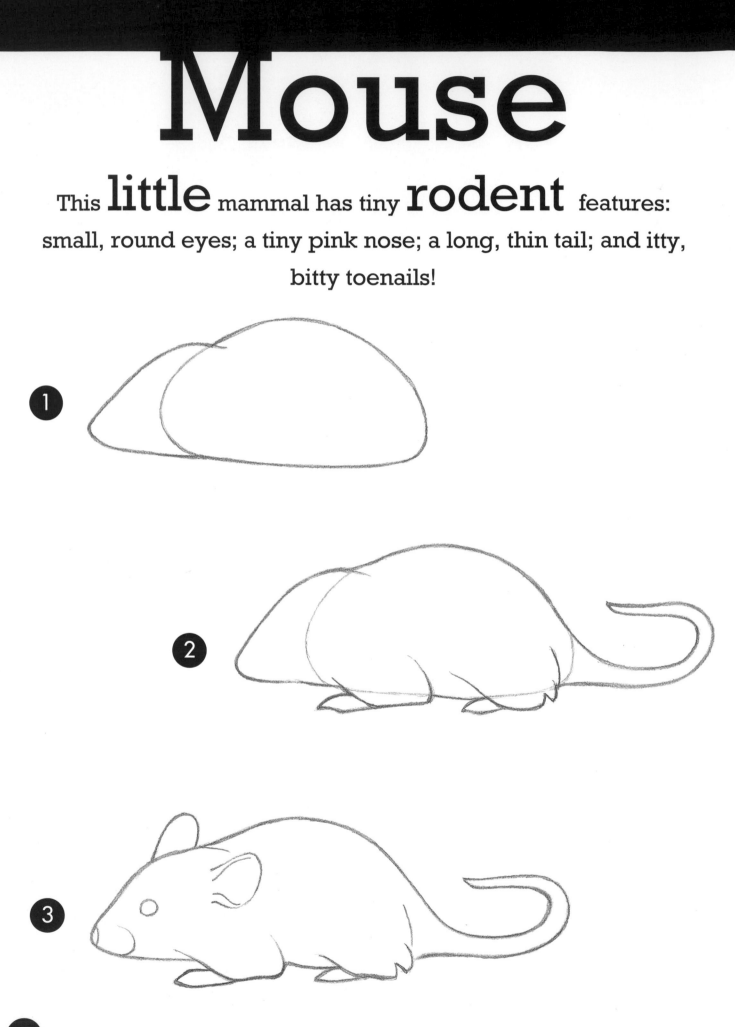

4

5

YUM YUM!

A mouse's front teeth keeps growing throughout its life, so it must constantly gnaw on things to wear down the teeth. This isn't hard to do, as mice will eat almost anything, from plants and insects to human food.

Ferret

With its slim body and small head, the ferret looks similar to a cat! But its rounded ears and masked markings distinguish it from most pets.

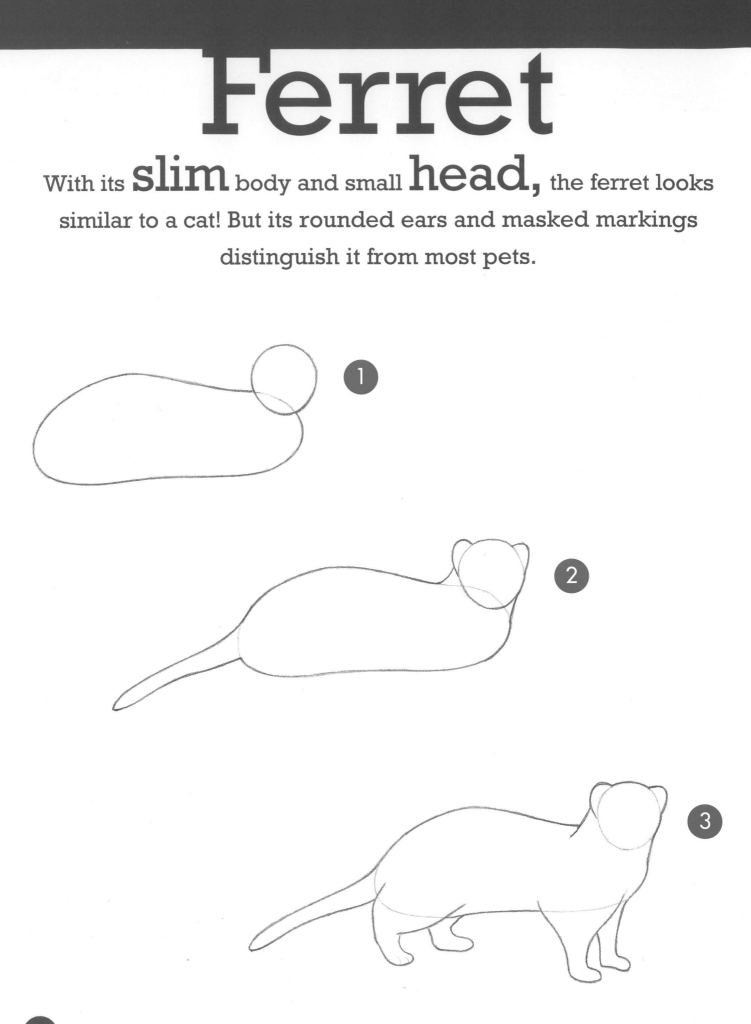

Ferrets have been *domesticated* for even longer than cats have. Yet the approximately 8 million domestic ferrets in the United States aren't officially recognized as pets by any state government, and it's illegal to own these furry friends in the state of California!

Percheron

The **unfeathered** Percheron is a **heavy** breed. Despite its size, it has the elegance of its Arabian ancestors.

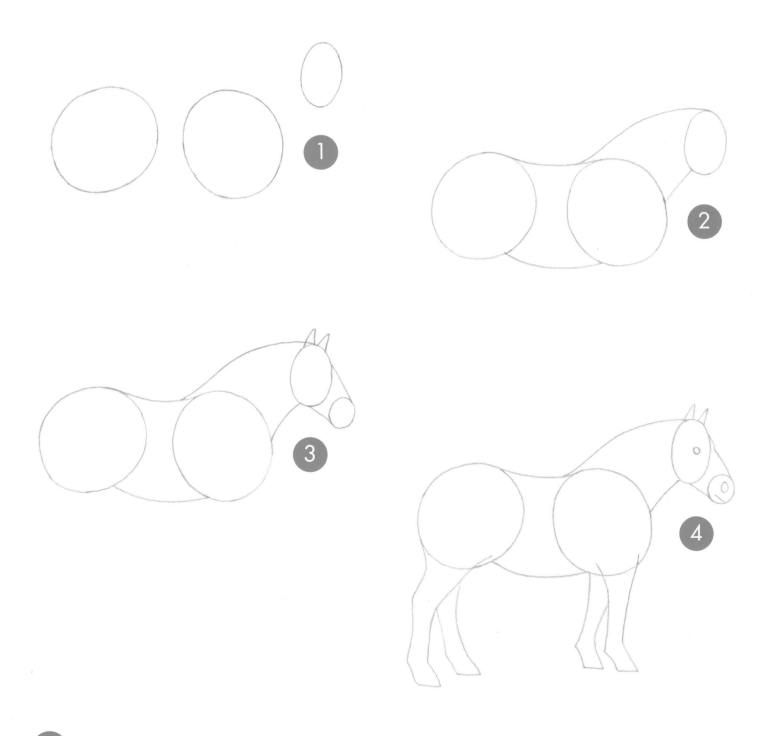

FUN FACT

Three of the *foals* recorded in the first American Percheron stud book in 1876 were fathered by a French horse named Diligence, who reportedly sired more than 400 foals in the United States.

5

6

7

Betta

Male **fighting fish** are known for their large, colorful fins, which they proudly display when they meet another male fish!

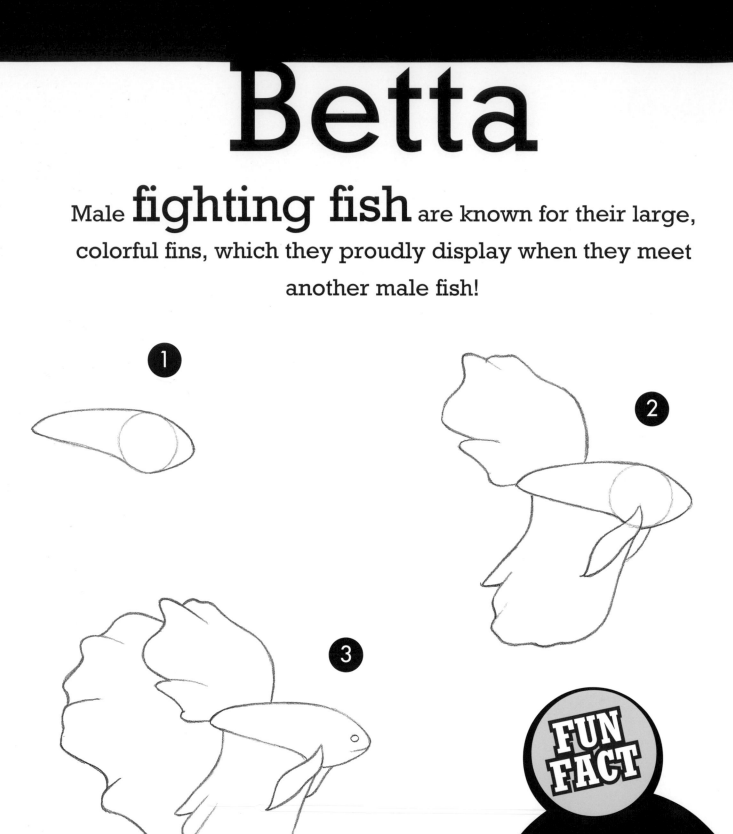

FUN FACT

Is there an aquarium at your dentist's office? Studies show that aquariums are relaxing and can lower the stress level of patients who are waiting for painful dental procedures.

Quick Quiz Answer: A male Betta.

American Saddlebred

This **high-spirited** horse shows off its **proud** style with a high-flying tail and a prancing step!

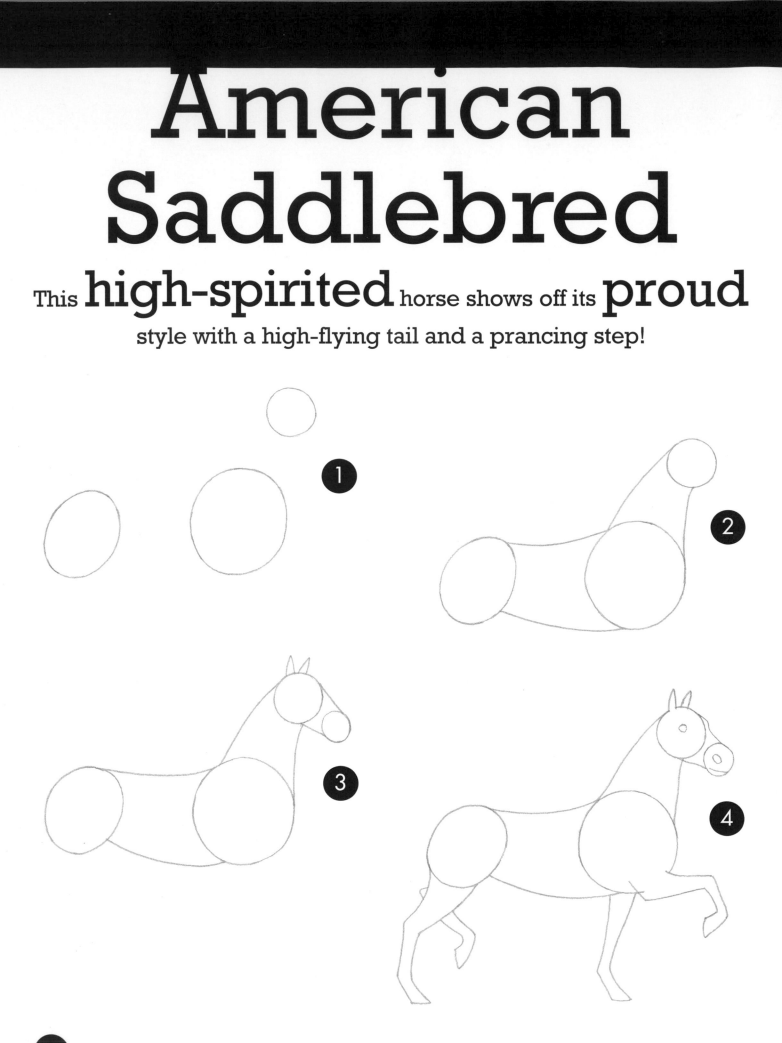

5

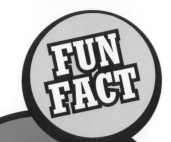
6

7

Cockatiel

The cockatiel's **crown** of feathers **stands up** when the bird is excited, but it lies flat and curls at the end when the bird is calm.

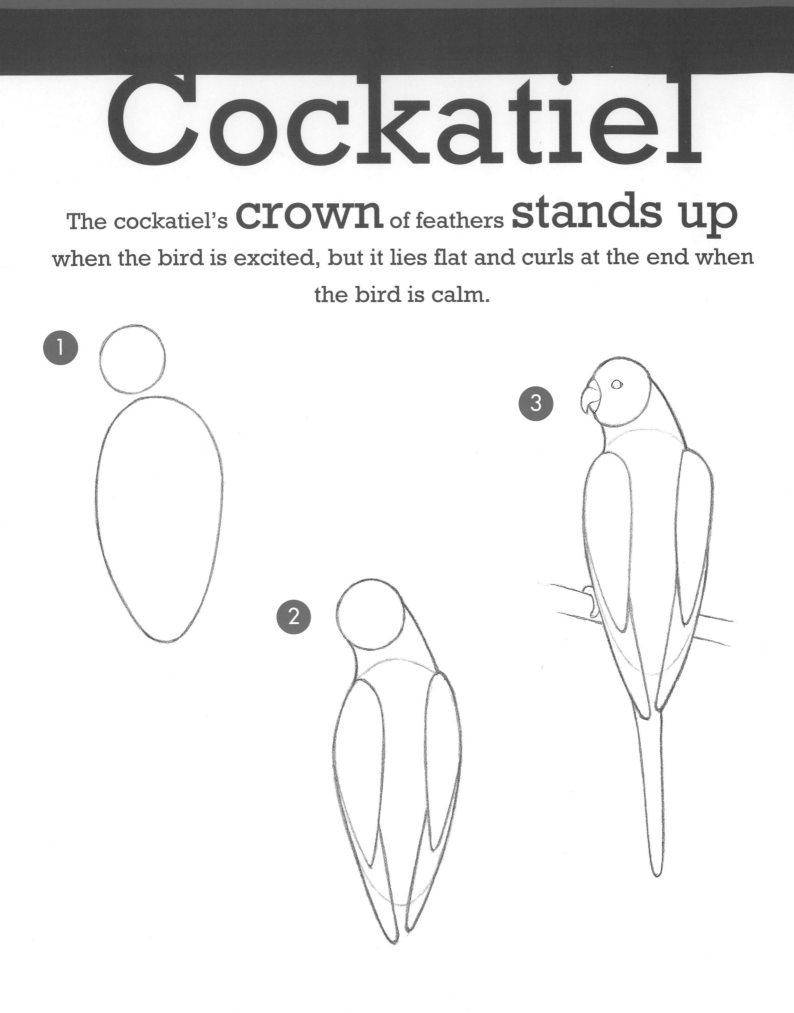

4

5

Because it's a social bird, your cockatiel needs a lot of attention, so the more you talk to, pet, and play with it, the better. Your cockatiel might even enjoy having a pet of its own! Experts say canaries make good pets for cockatiels. But don't expect your 'tiel to take care of the canary's feeding and clean-up; those will be your responsibilities!

Dog

A **Rottweiler** has a thick, stocky body and a **big** head. Draw this powerful dog with strong legs, a square jaw, and a straight back.

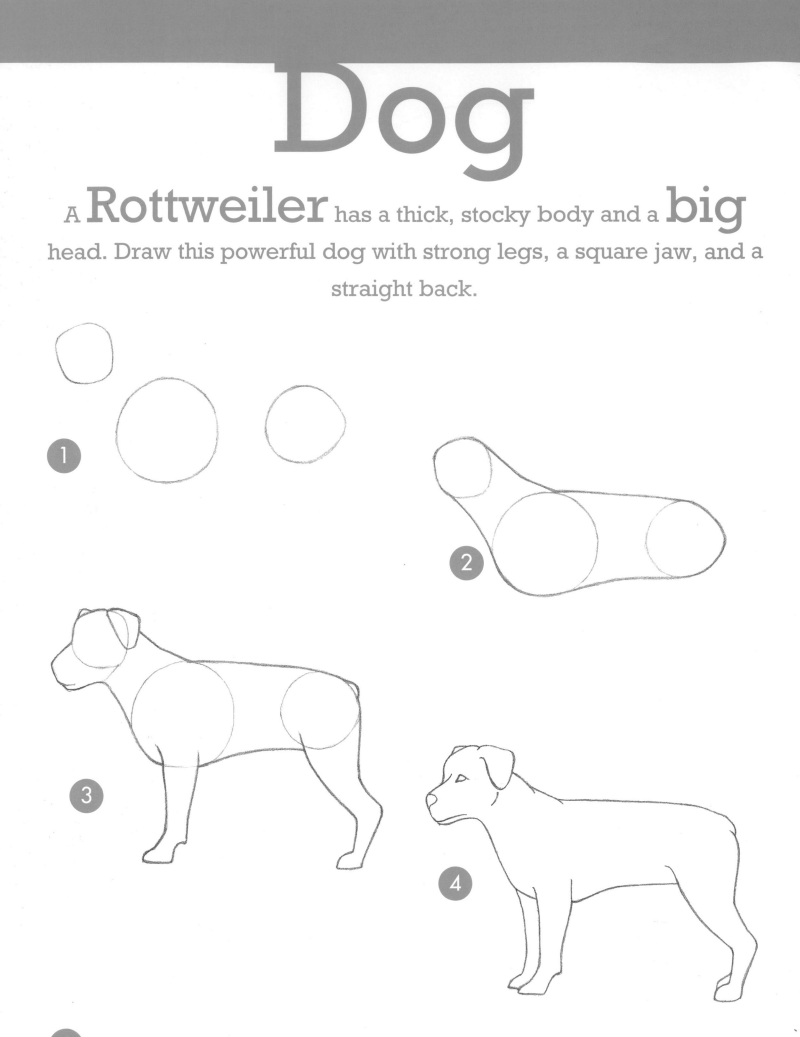

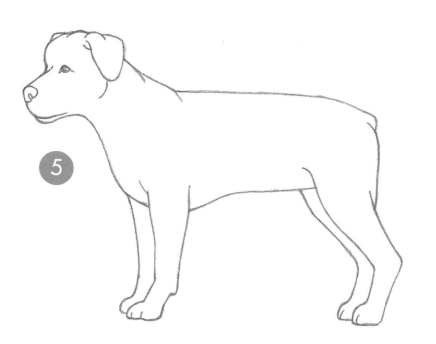

5

6

Iguana

When you draw this **scaly,** sun-loving **reptile,** be sure to make its tail longer than its head and body combined!

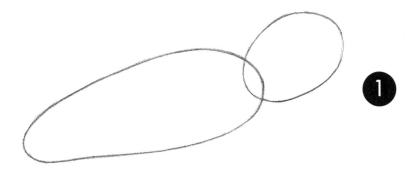

1

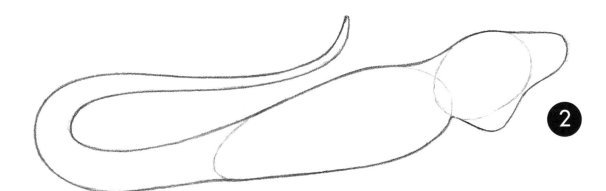

2

3

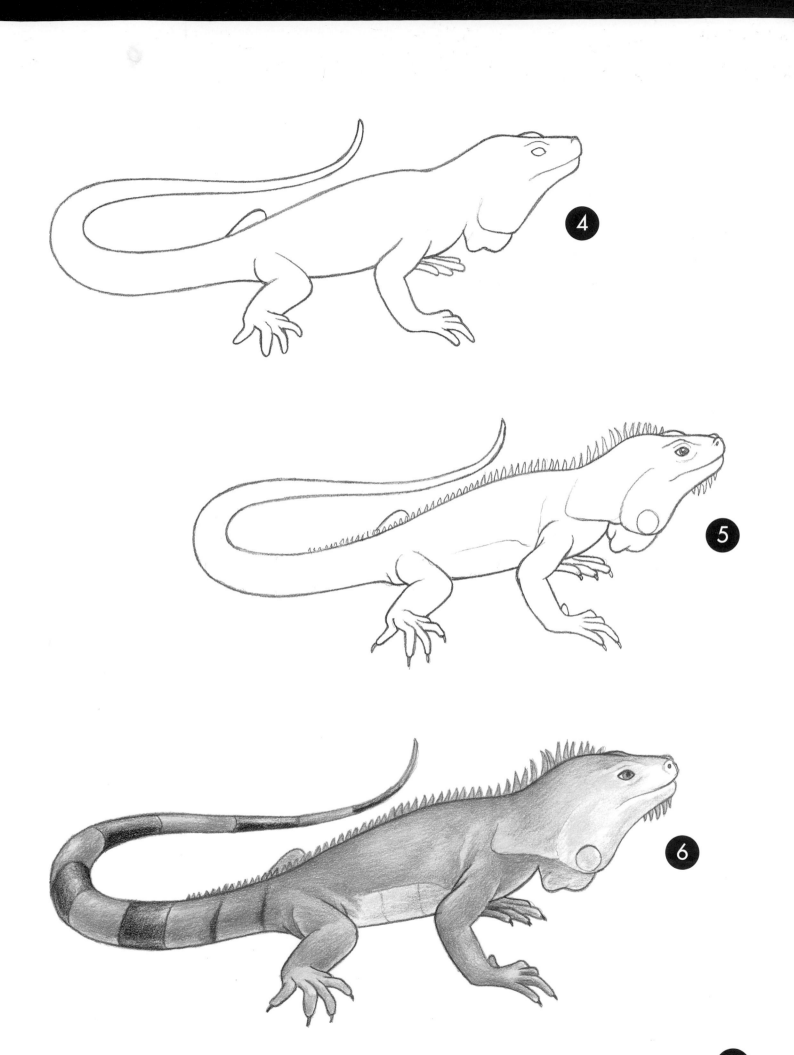

Shetland Pony

A **favorite** breed of pony lovers, the **adorable** Shetland is tiny but tough, with a round belly and short, stocky legs.

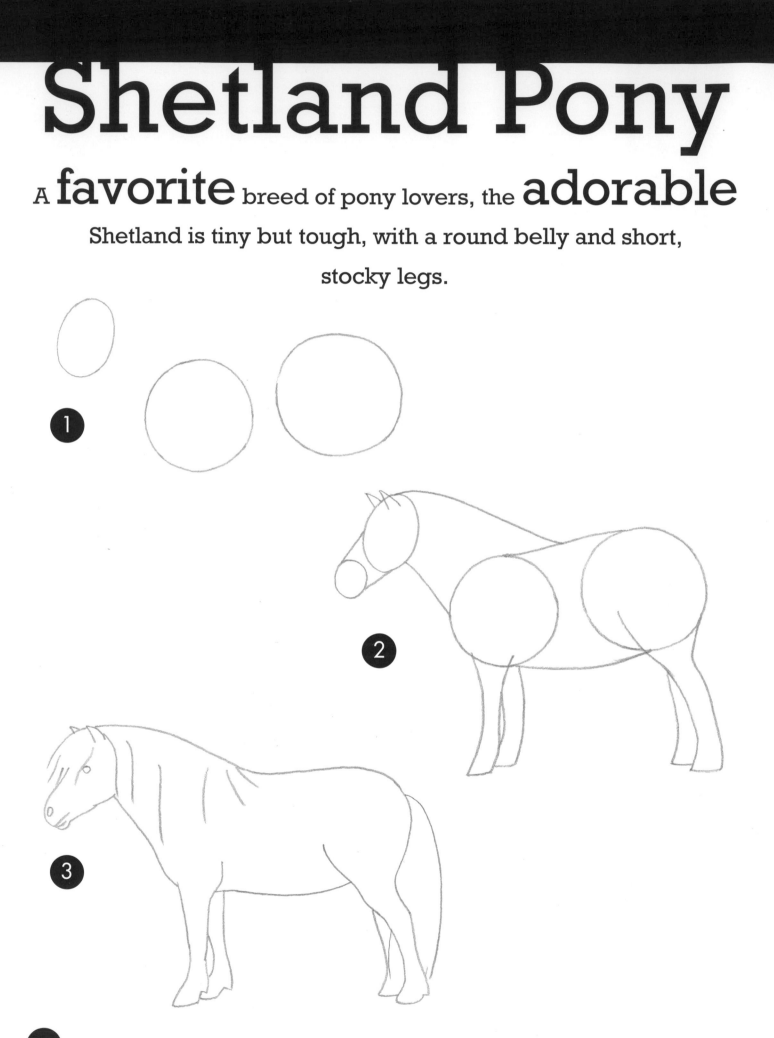

The Shetland Pony is the strongest equine for its size. A native to the Shetland Islands off the northern coast of Scotland, this pony was trained to carry heavy loads of peat and seaweed. The Shetland was also used to haul ore carts in coal mines.

Tropical Fish

Why stop at one fish when you can draw a whole aquarium?
Fill the water with Yellow Tangs, Moorish Idols, Blowfish, and more!

Short-Haired Cat

It's easy to **spot** this **feline's** shape because of its short coat! Start drawing this regal Bengal's body with a tall bean shape.

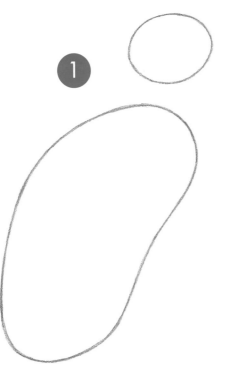

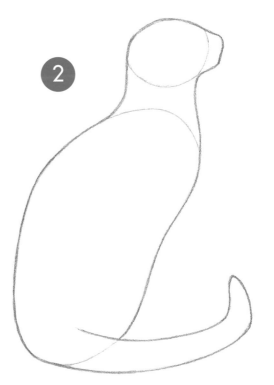

The first house cats were descendants of African and European wild cats! So don't be surprised if you see a resemblance between your kitty and the big cats at the zoo.

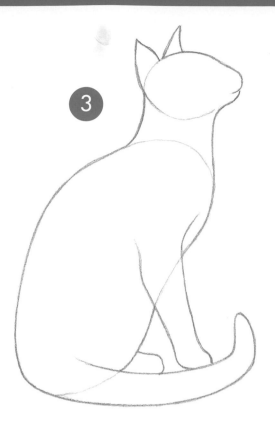

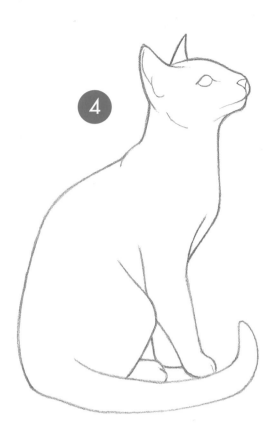

Parakeets

This **pair** of parakeets starts out with **similar** shapes, but the birds aren't identical. Look for the differences as you draw.

You can determine the gender of your parakeet by looking at its *cere*, or the bump above its beak. Male parakeets have bluish ceres and females have brownish ones. Males are more talkative and females like to chew stuff!

4

5

American Quarter Horse

With its **muscular** hindquarters and **powerful** shoulders, this Western horse can sprint like an Olympian and stop on a dime!

Morgan

Small but super **strong** and hardy, the Morgan has a draft horse's muscular hindquarters but thinner legs and an elegant face.

Quick Quiz Answer: True! However, it takes longer for a horse's eyes to adjust between light and dark.

5

QUICK QUIZ!

TRUE or FALSE?
A horse can see better at night than a human.

The answer is at the bottom of the opposite page.

6

FUN FACT

All Morgans are the descendants of the legendary Justin Morgan horse. Originally named Figure, the colt was later referred to by his owner's name and became famous for his feats outperforming much larger workhorses and racehorses. However, his finest feature was his powerful genes; all of his offspring inherited his appearance and abilities no matter what type of mare was bred to him!

Goldfish

Go Fish,

Like a game of **Go Fish,** drawing this goldfish is as simple as can be! Begin with an egg shape for the body, and then add the flowing fins!

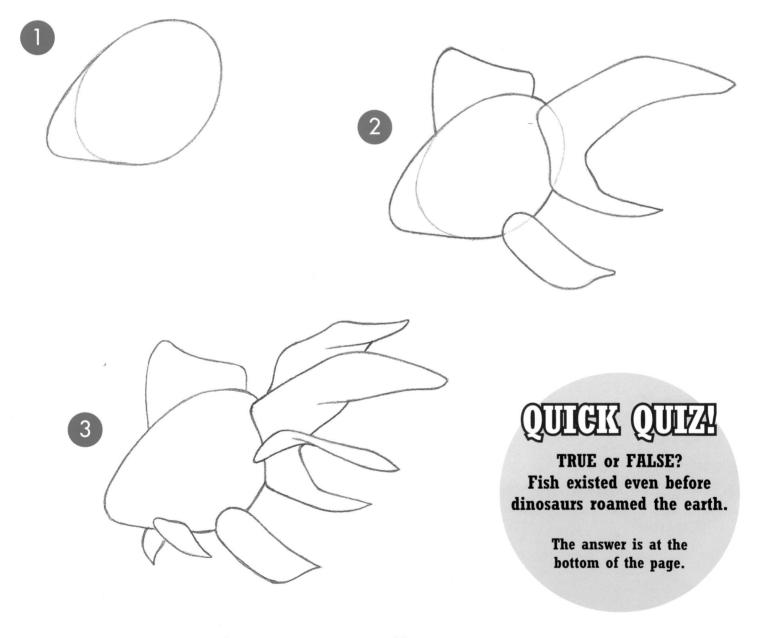

QUICK QUIZ!

TRUE or FALSE?
Fish existed even before dinosaurs roamed the earth.

The answer is at the bottom of the page.

Quick Quiz Answer: True! Some fish species were alive over 450 million years ago, whereas the first dinosaurs appeared about 200 million years later.

50

4

5

The most common name for pet goldfish in the United States is "Jaws." But Jaws isn't likely to respond to its name—or even remember it. The average memory span of a goldfish is only 3 seconds!

Snake

S-s-s-start with two oval shapes to **snake** yourself into position to draw this slithery coiled Python.

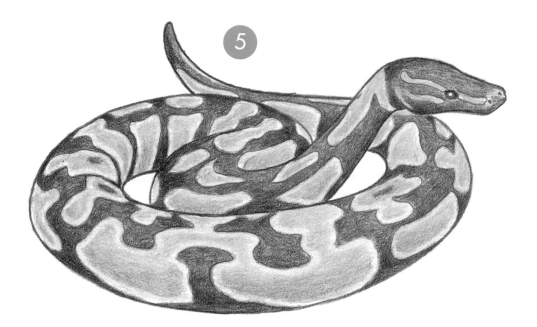

5

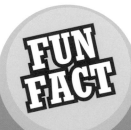

FUN FACT

The python wraps around its prey, constricts its meal, and swallows it whole, head first. It can take up to several weeks for the python to digest a large meal, but this snake can wait a few months before its next feeding.

Horses in Action

Whether **working** or **playing**, horses and people have been partners for thousands of years! Try your hand at drawing these active horses as they run, jump, and show off their skills!

Sliding stop

Racing

Playing polo

Jumping

Dressage

Harness racing

Pot-Bellied Pig

"Porkers" like this one love to **pig** out, so it's no surprise that this swine's most recognizable feature is its big round belly.

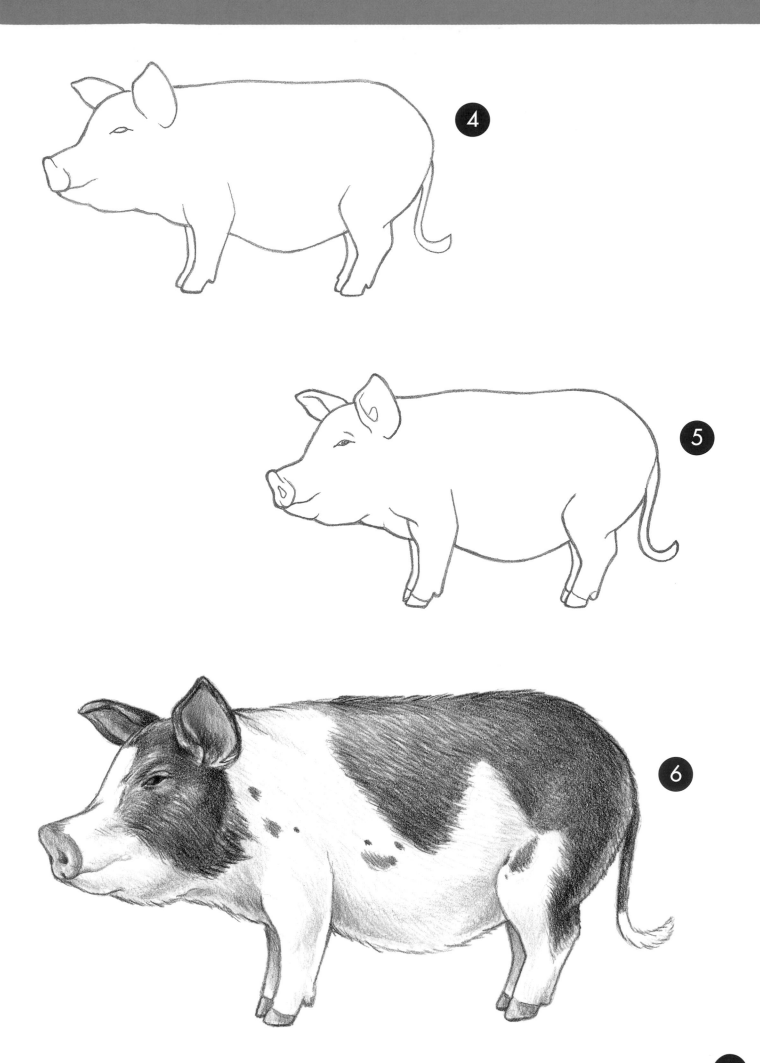

Friesian

Rapunzel would **envy** the long, flowing **locks** of this solid black Friesian—a heavy draft horse from the Netherlands.

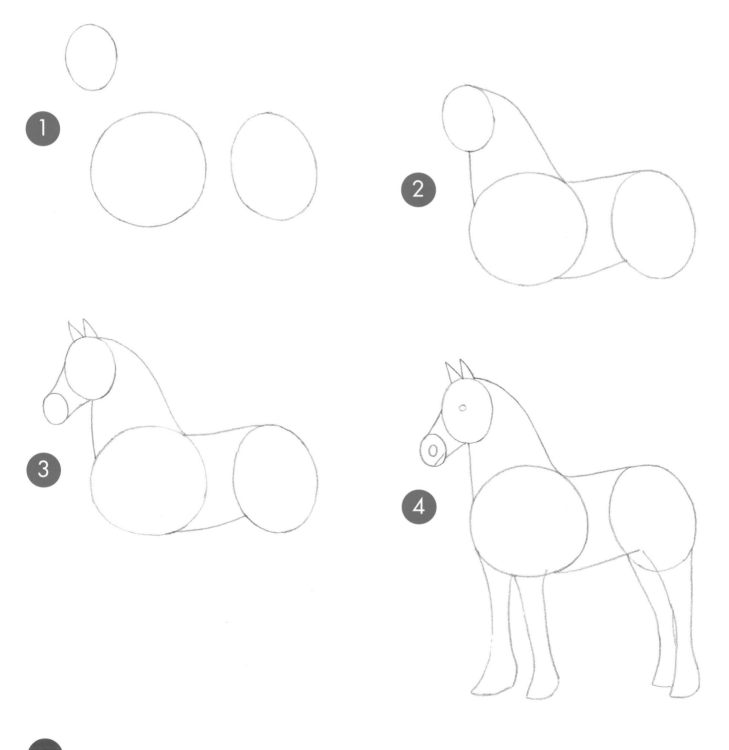

5

6

7

Hermit Crab

Like all **hermits,** this crab prefers to be **alone.** And there's no better place to retreat from the world than inside a shell!

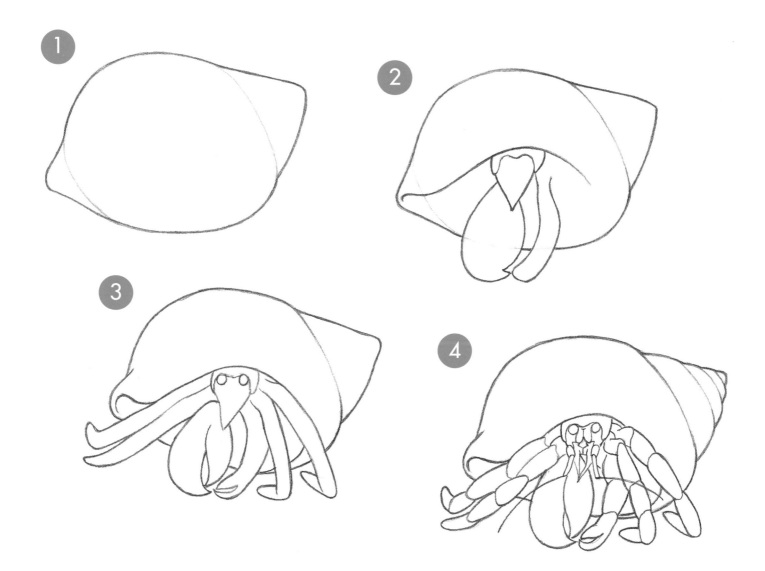

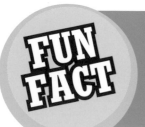

5

VERY CRABBY!

Hermit crabs aren't terribly friendly about sharing their space with others. If two of these crabs encounter one another, watch the claws fly: The hermits will battle it out until one falls out of its shell.

Appaloosa

The **easy-going** Appaloosa is awash in **spots!**
Along with its frosted coat pattern, it has a multi-colored tail.

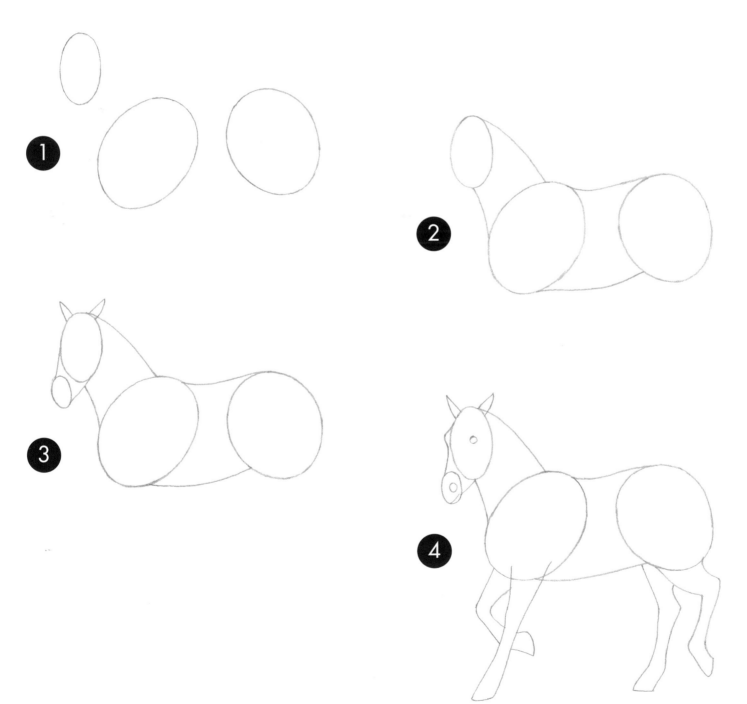

5

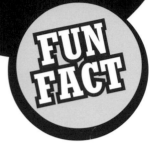

The first horses in the United States arrived in 1493. By 1780, most Native American tribes had horses, including the Nez Percé of the West. Expert horsemen, the Nez Percé selectively bred spotted horses, which later became the Appaloosa breed.

FUN FACT

6

7

Tarantula

An **arachnid** is a different kind of **"furry"** friend! This spider has eight shaggy legs and two shorter "arms" in front of its body.

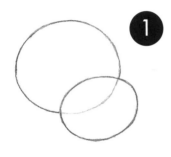

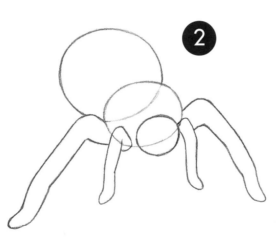

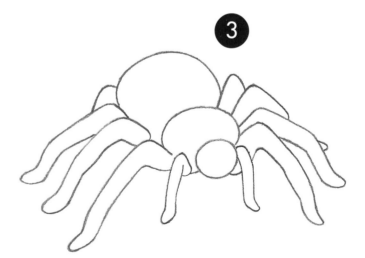

Quick Quiz Answer: A tarantula bite is no more dangerous than a bee sting, unless a person is allergic.

FUN FACT

Tarantulas are the only spiders that aren't able to spin webs strong enough to support their own weight.

Highland Pony

This **sure-footed** Scottish pony has the **build** of a draft horse, with soft, silky feathers on its lower legs.

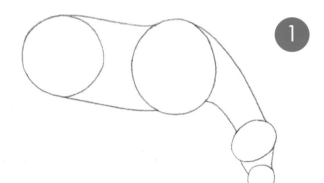

1

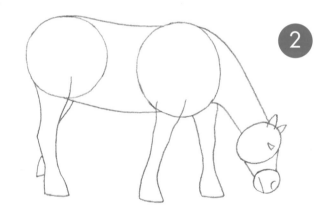

2

3

4

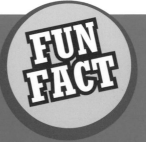

Highland ponies are well adapted to Scotland's extreme climates and can survive outside in all weather conditions. Their winter coat is thick and provides plenty of insulation against the cold. Then in the spring, they shed this layer of fur to reveal a sleek and smooth summer coat. These ponies are sturdy and versatile, great for a range of activities, such as packing, hunting, driving, jumping, and long-distance riding.

Tortoise

This **shell-back** moves **slowly** because it takes its home wherever it goes! Its four thick, strong legs have to work hard.

5

COOL MOVES

Tortoises don't have teeth. They use the sharp edges of their mouths to bite on plants that grow low on the ground, such as shrubs, grasses, and cactus. Some tortoises also eat insects and small animals. This slow-moving reptile spends most of its day browsing for food and slipping into cool burrows when the sun gets too hot.

Thoroughbred

The **fastest** breed in the world, the **athletic** and courageous Thoroughbred can run and jump for miles and miles!

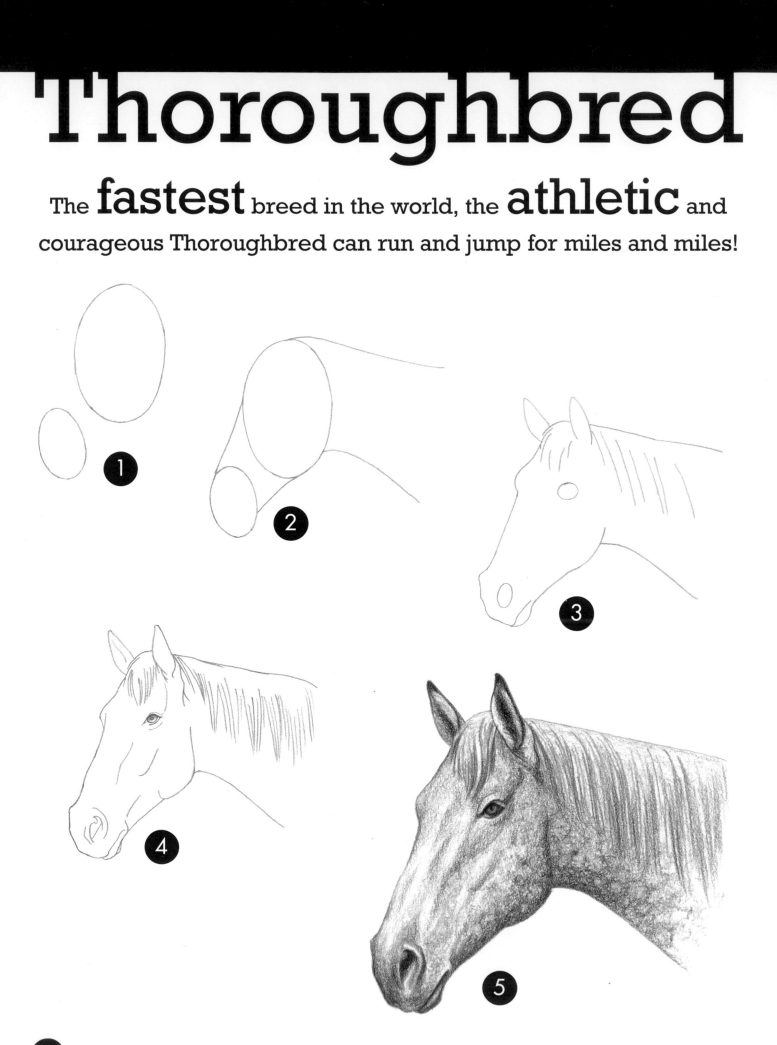

Kathiawari

This narrowly built horse from **India** has distinctive **ears** that curve inward until their tips actually touch!

① ② ③ ④

⑤

FUN FACT

This horse is small, but it's also tough, which is why the Kathiawari is a favorite of tent-pegging athletes. Originally a way to practice wild boar hunting, tent pegging is now a popular sport in India. To play the game, an athlete rides to the center of an arena and, while on horseback, uses the tip of a lance to pick up a small wooden block—or peg. Picking up the peg earns the rider half a point; picking up the peg and carrying it to the opposite corner of the arena earns a full point.

Long-Haired Cat

Is there a **body** under that **fluff?** Of course! But for a purr-fect Persian portrait, just draw the shapes that you can see!

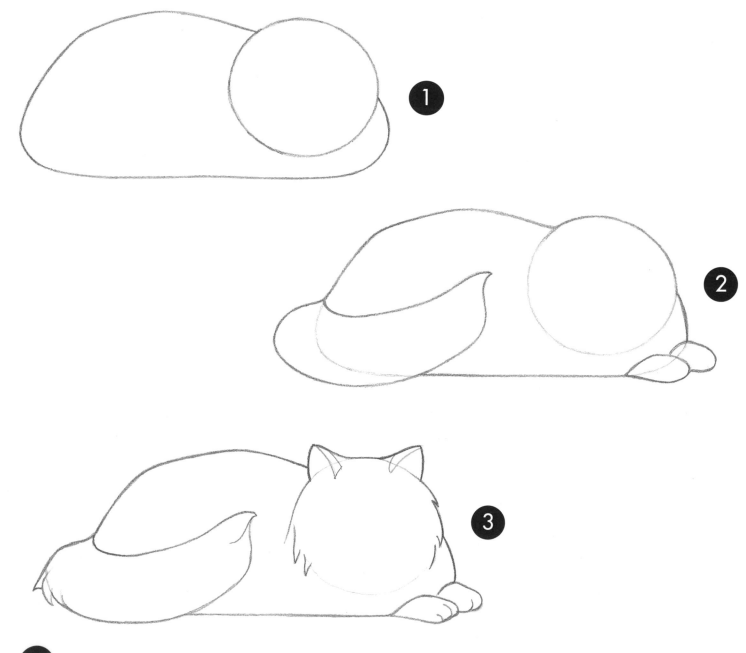

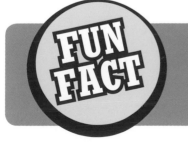

Paso Fino

Also called a "stepping" horse for its natural, lively gait, the Paso has long hind legs and pasterns and very flexible joints.

5

6

QUICK QUIZ!

Question: What does *paso fino* **mean?**

The answer is at the bottom of the opposite page.

FUN FACT

The Paso Fino is known for its smooth, four-beat gait that can naturally be performed since birth. Its easy, rhythmic gait provides riders with unequaled comfort, and its refined head and graceful neck give the Paso Fino a proud and stylish look.

Guinea Pig

This little **cowlicked furball** is also called a
"cavy." It may be the only pet with permanent "bedhead"!

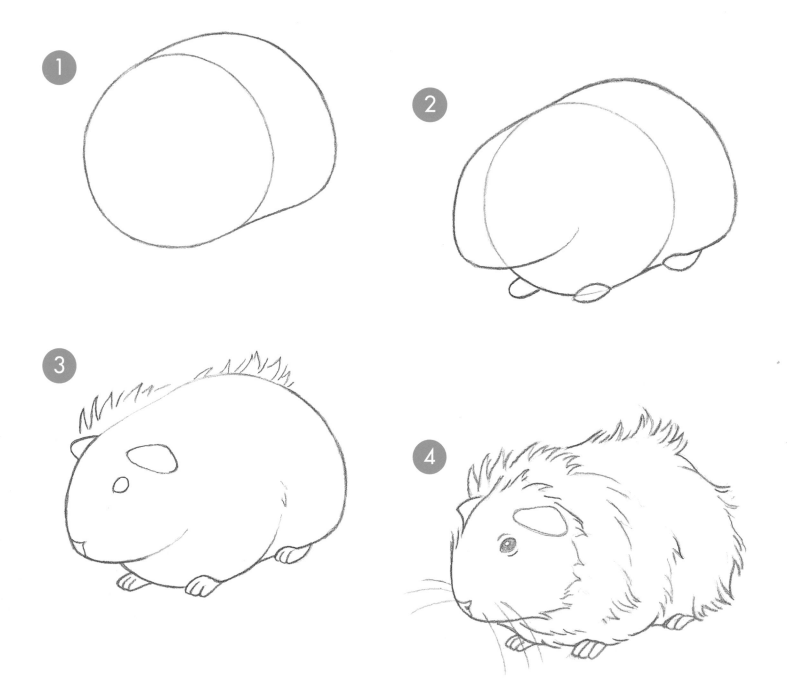

QUICK QUIZ!

Question: What animal is the guinea pig most closely related to: a pig, a rat, or a rabbit?

The answer is at the bottom of the opposite page.

5

FUN FACT

At birth, guinea pigs already have hair and their eyes are open. These little critters originally came from South America, where they were used for food. They are still regarded as a delicacy there today.

Rocky Mountain Pony

Its dappled **chocolate** coloring and **creamy** mane and tail make this pretty pony a one-of-a-kind sensation!

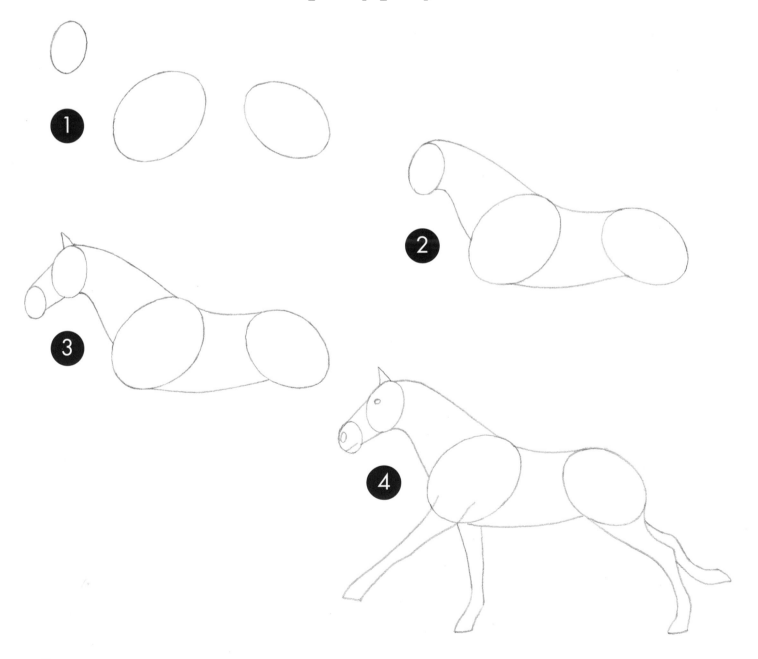

Glossary

Amphibious (AM-fib-ee-iss) - To be able to live on land and in water.

Arachnid (u-RACK-nid) - An insect-like creature with eight legs, such as a spider, scorpion, or tick.

Constrict (cun-STRICT) - To squeeze or compress.

Crustacean (crus-TAY-shin) - An animal that usually lives in water and has a hard outer shell and several pairs of legs.

Domesticate (do-MESS-ti-cayt) - To train a wild animal to live with or work for humans.

Exoskeleton (EK-so-ske-le-tin) - A hard, outer covering, such as the shell of a turtle, crab, or tarantula.

Foal (rhymes with hole) - Young horse up to one year of age.

Gait (GAYT) - A pattern of footsteps that a horse uses to move, such as a canter, trot, or gallop.

Habitat (HAB-i-tat) - Where an animal lives, such as the ocean or desert.

Mammal (MA-mol) - A warm-blooded animal that has hair and feeds its young milk, such as a human or dog.

Nocturnal (nock-TURN-ul) - If an animal is nocturnal, it means that it sleeps or hides during the day and only comes out at night.

Predator (PRE-da-tur) - An animal that kills and eats other animals.

Withers (WI-thurs) - Point at the bottom of a horse's neck from which the height of the horse is measured.